# Adam Smith
## Kirkcaldy's most famous citizen

It was decided to write this short boo̤ ̤̤̤̤̤ Adam Smith's Kirkcaldy, because there is so little in this town directly connected with Kirkcaldy's greatest citizen yet many parts of the town were here in his time. Copies of his two great works, with a few relics of Adam Smith which have survived may be seen in Kirkcaldy Museum.

Adam Smith is Kirkcaldy's most famous citizen, born here over 278 years ago. He is regarded by the American author Michael Hart as the 33rd most important person ever to have lived. Kirkcaldy should indeed be proud of its most famous citizen and be prepared to welcome the many would-be tourists, especially the Japanese who worship Adam Smith, the founder father of modern economics.

Adam Smith was the only child of Jane Douglas of Strathhendry Castle, Leslie, Fife, the second wife of Adam Smith W.S., Controller of Customs and Judge Advocate of Scotland. He was responsible for all taxes and duties between Aberdour and Largo. Sadly he died before his son was born.

Adam Smith was born in Kirkcaldy in 1723, in a house close to where the entrance to the Mercat is today. He was baptised in the Parish Church of St Brisse on June 5 1723, with James Oswald of Dunnikier House, now known as Path House, as witness.

When Adam Smith was four years old and was staying at Strathhendry Castle, he was stolen by the gypsies. The alarm was soon raised, his uncle rode off in search of him and he was found not far away with the gypsies, who were relieved to be rid of a small, ungamely, squawking little boy. No harm had been done.

2

**Adam Smith from a painting** Reproduced by kind permission from the Scottish National Portrait Gallery. Artist unknown

**Dunnikier House**, known as Path House after James Townsend Oswald built the new Dunnikier House, now a Hotel.

Adam Smith spent many years in Kirkcaldy, until December 1777 when he was appointed Commissioner of Customs for Scotland, and went to live in Panmure House in Edinburgh's High Street. He died in Edinburgh aged 67 in 1790 and is buried in Canongate Kirkyard.

Adam was educated at the Burgh School, then in Hill Street and from there at the young age of 14, not unusual in those days, he went to Glasgow University. From there he was awarded a Snell Exhibition to Balliol College, Oxford. Here he was self-taught for in his words:- *"in the University of Oxford the greater part of the publick professors have for these many years given up altogether even the pretence of teaching".* Their income, unlike that of the Scottish Professors, was independent of teaching responsibilities. He stayed in Oxford for 6 years from 1740-46. The Scots were not popular there and Adam was not always well and in addition to bronchitis, he suffered from something akin to St Vitus dance, a facial tic. He was lonely and homesick, missing his Scottish home. The Snell Exhibition was for those intending to join the Episcopal Church but after the '45 Uprising, Episcopalians and Catholics were not allowed in Scotland, to worship in groups. However Adam Smith no longer wished to enter the Church and so he resigned his Exhibition. He was a Royalist and likewise Glasgow University was loyal to the Hanoverians.

In 1746 Adam Smith returned to Kirkcaldy. From 1748 until 1751 he gave a series of lectures at Edinburgh University where he met David Hume, the well-known philosopher. He gained popularity and in 1752 was appointed to the Chair of Logic at Glasgow University. The next year he became Professor of Moral Philosophy. His lectures were always said to be interesting and he drew his examples from everyday life. He spent over nine years at Glasgow University until he received an offer that interested him greatly, for he was invited to be travelling tutor to the young Duke of Buccleugh and accompanied him on a tour of the Continent

**Burgh School**

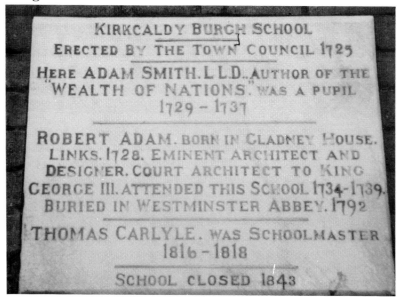

KIRKCALDY BURGH SCHOOL
ERECTED BY THE TOWN COUNCIL 1725

HERE ADAM SMITH. L L.D..AUTHOR OF THE
WEALTH OF NATIONS. WAS A PUPIL
1729 – 1737

ROBERT ADAM. BORN IN GLADNEY HOUSE.
LINKS. 1728. EMINENT ARCHITECT AND
DESIGNER. COURT ARCHITECT TO KING
GEORGE III. ATTENDED THIS SCHOOL 1734-1739.
BURIED IN WESTMINSTER ABBEY. 1792

THOMAS CARLYLE. WAS SCHOOLMASTER
1816 – 1818

SCHOOL CLOSED 1843

**Plaque in Hill Street**

visiting France and Switzerland for three years. After a few months in London on his return, he came back to Kirkcaldy and stayed with his mother at what is now 220 High Street.

Adam Smith remained in Kirkcaly until 1773, studying the nail-makers of Pathhead and preparing his most famous work, "An Inquiry into the Nature and Causes of the Wealth of Nations". Industrial nailers were still making nails the old fashioned way, but with the newly opened Carron Iron Company in 1759, new methods were to be adopted. The nailers of Pathhead were not flexible enough to accept new methods of manufacture and so later went out of business.

Adam Smith was very methodical about his writings and continually edited his work until he was satisfied with the result. "The Wealth of Nations" was first published in 1776 and was an immediate success. There were five editions during his lifetime.

Adam Smith was often lost in his thoughts and early one Sunday morning he set off down his garden towards the shore in his night clothes. When he came to, he heard the church bells ringing; he had walked to Dunfermline twelve miles along the Turnpike Road!

In 1773 he went to London with the unpublished "Wealth of Nations" returning in December 1777 to take up his new appointment as Commissioner of Customs for Scotland. He never married and so he, with his mother and cousin Jane Douglas, moved to Edinburgh, where he founded the Oyster Club and had Sunday evening suppers for his friends. His mother died in 1784, six years before him and his cousin Jane four years later. He was devastated. Before he died at the age of 67, in 1790, he had ordered some of his trusted friends sadly to burn all his unfinished works. Adam Smith is buried in Canongate Kirkyard Edinburgh. Among his friends and contemporaries were James Oswald of Dunnikier/Path House and his brother John, who later became

**Ravenscraig Castle c 18th Century**

**St Serf's Church, Dysart c 1900, below the Old Manse and Bay Horse Inn** with lintel "My hoip is in the Lord 1582"

the Bishop of Raphoe (Ireland); Robert Adam the famous architect; John Dryburgh, son of the Rev. Dryburgh of Kirkcaldy Parish Church, later Minister of the Tron Church, Edinburgh and later still Moderator of the Church of Scotland and also David Hume (1711-76), Edinburgh Philosopher. Dugald Stewart of Edinburgh (1753-1838) was also his friend and states that in his younger years Adam Smith was attracted to a young lady, whom he did not name. Sadly Adam Smith was not successful in pressing his suit and it is said that he never got over this romance and was not involved with any other ladies.

Adam Smith produced two great works "The Theory of Moral Sentiments", published in 1759 and "An Inquiry into the Nature and Causes of the Wealth of Nations", which is still popular today. His works were intended as a trilogy with the third volume to be on 'Law and Government', but this never appeared and most of his papers would have been destroyed when all his manuscripts, except those he was satisfied were complete, were burned in 1790, on his orders.

However some of his lecture notes on Jurisprudence turned up among the archives of Glasgow University in 1895 and were published in 1958. A further addition with more notes was published in 1978.

In Glasgow University there is a 'Special Collection', of 240 documents, gifted by Rev. Dr David Douglas Bannerman, descendent of David Douglas, later Lord Reston, cousin of Adam Smith. More are being added to this collection from auctions, as extra articles appear.

**Adam Smith believed in the principles of Free Trade, free from government control or tariffs. He believed that Division of Labour was a more efficient method of producing manufactured goods.**

**Entrance to Panmure House,
High Street, Edinburgh**

**Old Parish
Church c1860**
(Rebuilt 1808)

# Kirkcaldy in Adam Smith's Day

In 1707 there was the Union of the Parliaments and many new taxes and duties were introduced into Scotland which affected adversely much of the Scots' trade with the Continent. Earlier the Covenanting movement had reduced the number of both men and ships in Kirkcaldy and was followed by the Civil War which again cost Kirkcaldy and Scotland contributions, which included the premature Coronation in 1651 in Scone of Charles II, although he was not restored to the British monarchy until 1660.

Kirkcaldy in Adam Smith's day, according to the Old Statistical Account (OSA) written by the Rev. Thomas Fleming of the Parish Church in 1795, (uncle of the child poet, Marjory Fleming) was *"but one long street with a few lanes opening on each side of it"*. The population was said to be 2607 souls of whom 250 were scholars.

Kirkcaldy had been made a Royal Burgh in 1644 by Charles I when at the same time he gave nearly 9 acres of common land known as the South Commonty to the town. It ran from John Louden's Wynd (no longer there) by the Burleigh Burn (culverted) to George Burn Wynd. Later the remaining part of this land became known as Volunteers' Green, but by 1870 the amount of ground was only about an acre, and later it was further reduced to half an acre, in two parts, separated by 600 yards/550 metres.

There was the Parish of Abbotshall to the south of Kirkcaldy, which included Linktown and of Dunnikier or Pathhead to the north of the Den Burn. About 2 miles along the coast was the Royal Burgh of Dysart, which included, Pathhead, Gallatown and Sinclairtown. In 1876 Linktown, Pathhead, Sinclairtown and Gallatown joined the Royal Burgh of Kirkcaldy and Royal Dysart followed in 1930.

**Gladney House**

**Lions' House c 1900**

Linen was the main industry of Kirkcaldy and until the turn of the century, when steam-power was gradually introduced, the power source was from water. At this time there were 250 hand-looms in Kirkcaldy, 300 in Abbotshall and 100 in Dysart.

Tanning of hides and skins was Kirkcaldy's second industry. Nail-making was the main industry of Pathhead and part of Gallatown. Saltpans had died off with the new excise duties and taxes but as coal became plentiful again, the salt industry revived, mainly owned by Mr Oswald of Dunnikier. Bucket patts, reservoirs for retaining sea water at low tide, remained on the shore until the commencement of the building of the sea wall in 1922.

Ship building started in 1778 after America had won Independence (1776), so British ships were no longer built across the Atlantic where wood was plentiful and cheap. Turnpike roads had been built with Toll Bars to extract tolls from road users for the upkeep of the new roads. Transport would be by coach, on horseback, on foot or by boat. There were busy harbours both at Kirkcaldy and Dysart and travel by ship was often quicker and easier than by road as the latter were few, in poor condition, and often unsafe.

The Gregorian Calendar was adopted in 1752 replacing the Julian Calendar. and taking 11 days from the month of September The Scots were furious and shouted "Give us back our 11 days".

Besides the Parish Church there was the new Parish Church of Abbotshall built in 1674 (congregation established 1650). The Secession of 1733 had established a congregation just south of the Kirkcaldy boundary, in Linktown, where the first Bethelfield Church was built in 1737 and was later rebuilt a little further inland. In 1747 the anti-burghers split off from the Bethelfield Burghers and worshipped in a barn near the Harbour, later moving into Dunnikier/Pathhead and building their Dunnikier Church around 1765 with Dunnikier House, later known as the Path House, the

**Raith House**

**Whyte House 1999**

home of the minister. Manses for ministers were not often provided by congregations until the end of the 18th Century.

Adam Smith may have left Kirkcaldy at the time John Paul Jones, Scots born founder of the American Navy and privateer attempted to plunder Kirkcaldy in 1778, but the town was saved following Rev. Shirra's prayer meeting on the shore which resulted in a fierce gale chasing John Paul Jones away. The Lord had saved Kirkcaldy!! (See picture page 27)

At this time there were a few wealthy landowners in big houses, a small middle class of merchants, and many poor, living in hovels of rough stone and turf roofs. William Adam, father of Robert Adam, with William Robertson, had set up a Brick and Tile works in Linktown in 1714 and the better houses would be of brick and tile. *"The houses of Kirkcaldy are generally mean, awkwardly placed with their ends to the street and constructed without any regard to order or uniformity"*. OSA Window tax was bringing in money from the big houses and was not repealed until 1851.

In Adam Smith's day the following big houses were in existence:-
*15th Century Sailors' Walk and Ravenscraig Castle; 16th Century Merchant's House; Path House built in 1692 and then known as Dunnikier House; Raith House built in 1694; St Brycedale House built in 1785, better known as the Hunter Hospital. In Linktown, Gladney House was built in 1711 (demolished in 1930) and the Lions' House was built in 1778. (demolished c1914). It was 1790 before the new Dunnikier House, now a hotel, was built, also Balsusney House (demolished 1920), the Whyte House (under threat) and in the Links, Viewforth Tower (demolished in 1956).*

Dysart was about a mile from Ravenscraig Castle, which had been uninhabited since the late 17th Century, when the Sinclairs had built the more comfortable nearby dwelling house, the Hermitage.

Adam Smith Halls

**Bust of Adam Smith in Foyer of Adam Smith Theatre**

Sadly this house went on fire in 1722 and was rebuilt on site as Dysart House in 1726. The old Church of St Serf on the shore was getting cold and draughty so in 1802 it was replaced with Dysart Barony Church and shortly after a road was driven through the centre of old St Serf's Church making, a fast route for coal to reach the harbour. A year before Adam Smith was born, John Pitcairn (1722-1775) was born, in Dysart, in the Manse beside St Serf's Church, son of the minister Rev. David Pitcairn. He served as a Major with the Marines in America (War of Independence 1775-76), tried to prevent the outbreak of war at Lexington and was mortally wounded at Breed's or "Bunkers Hill". Perhaps they were acquainted?

In OSA 1795 eminent men were named as:- *Michael Scott 13th Century; George Gillespie 1613-49 Covenanting Minister, born and died in Kirkcaldy; Dr John Drysdale, Minister in Edinburgh born in Kirkcaldy 1718-1788; Mr James Oswald MP 1715-69 and Dr Adam Smith.* There was one MP for Kirkcaldy, Kinghorn, Burntisland and Dysart and 28 voters!! Money was the Scots Pound of which 12 were equal to an English pound.

Information on the birthplace of Adam Smith is sought after by many tourists to Kirkcaldy. By studying the 1824 map in the centre pages some idea can be had of Adam Smith's Langtoun.

# In the Steps of Adam Smith, the Trail

### The Trail starts at Kirkcaldy Museum and Art Gallery

Here there is a small collection of Adam Smith's mementoes including a first and fourth edition (each 2 volumes) of the "Wealth of Nations". The Trail points out some of the evidence left in Kirkcaldy of the town that Adam Smith would have known mainly during the period from 1766-73 when he lived at 220 High Street. Walk through the War Memorial Gardens towards the **Adam Smith Theatre** which was opened in 1899 as the Adam Smith

MAGISTER GEORGIUS GILLESPIE PASTOR EDINBURGENSIS IUVENILIBUS ANNIS RITU JM ANGLORUM PONTIFICIORUM TURMAM PROSTRAVIT: GLISCENTE ÆTATE, DELEGATUS CUM MANDATIS IN SYNODO ANGLICANA PRÆS ULEM E ANGLIA ERADICANDUM SINCERUM DEI CULTUM UNIFORMEM PROMOVENDUM CURAVIT ERAS TUM AARONIS GERMINANTE VIRGA CASTIGAVIT IN BAT RIAM REVERSUS FŒDIFRAGOS ANGLIAM BELLO LACESSEN TES LABEFACTAVIT SYNODI NATIONALIS ANNO 1648 EDINBURGI HABITÆ PRÆSES ELECTUS EXTREMAM PATRIÆ SUÆ OPERAM CUM LAUDE NAVAVIT CUMQUE OCULATUS TESTIS VIDISSET MALIGNANTIUM QUAM PRÆDIXERAT RUI NAM EODEM QUO FŒDUS TRIUM GENTIUM SOLENNE REN OVATUM FUIT DIE DECEDENS IN PACE ANNO ÆTATIS N GAUDIUM DOMINI INTRAVIT: INGENIO PROFUNDUS GENIO MITIS DISPUTATIONE ACUTUS ELOQUIO FACUN US ANIMO INVICTUS BONOS IN AMOREM, MALOS IN INVIDE AM OMNES IN SUI ADMIRATIONEM RAPUIT PATRE SUÆ OR NAMENTUM: TANTO PATRE DIGNA SOBOLES.

THIS TOMB BEING PULLED DOWN BY THE MALIGN IN FLUENCE OF ARCHBISHOP SHARP AFTER THE INTRO DUCTION OF PRÆLACY MR GEORGE GILLESPIE MINR OF THE GOSPEL AT STRATHMIGLO CAUSED IT TO BE REE RECTED IN HONOUR OF HIS SAID WORTHY GRAND FATHER WAS A STANDING MONUMENT OF DUTIFUL RE GARD TO HIS BLESSED MEMORY AN:DOM: 1746

This tomb being pulled
down by the malign
influence of Archbishop
Sharp after the intro-
-duction of praelacy.
Mr George Gillespie
Min. of the Gospel at
Strathmiglo caused it
to be reerected in
Honour of his said
worthy Grandfather
& as a standing
Monument of
dutiful regard to his
blessed Memory
An.Dom.1746

**George Gillespie Memorial
Stone inside south door
of Old Parish Church**

Robert Whyt 1701-1796 wife
Elizabeth Edmonstone 1716-1797
They are buried in the old Kirk with
5 of their 14 children

Rt. Hon. James Oswald 1715-1769
buried Westminster Abbery,
married in 1746 Elizabeth Townsend
of Huntingdon Hall 1699-1779.
(His wife was apparently 16 years
his senior and James Townsend
Oswald their only son was born
when she was 49!! (Oswald family tree)

**Inscriptions on some  contemporary  graves,  Old Kirk**

Halls, to commemorate the 100 years since the death of Adam Smith in 1790. A Committee had been set up by 54 year old Provost Michael Beveridge, donor of the Beveridge Park, who died in 1890, before the plans had finalised. It took several years before the Halls were ready to open which included the Beveridge Hall and Library. The Halls were opened in October 1899 by Andrew Carnegie of Skibo Castle, (Sutherland), Dunfermline born philanthropist (1835-1919).

## Kirk Wynd and Old Parish Church

Turn into St Brycedale Avenue, known before 1843 as Wemyss Place which connected with Wemyssfield, a Right of Way. Opposite the Police Station is Fife College built on the site of the High School which, as the Burgh School had moved from Hill Street into a new building in 1843 and after being extended remained here until the High School moved to new buildings on Dunnikier Way in 1958.

Turn right into Kirk Wynd after passing St Brycedale Church. On the opposite side of the road is the Manse of the Old Parish Church built in 1808 as was the Church, which except for the older tower, was rebuilt and opened in 1808. A church had been on this site since early times, first as a simple Culdee Cell and later as Roman Catholicism was introduced by Queen Margaret, as a Catholic Church. It was consecrated by Bishop David de Bernham in 1240 and known as the Church of St Brisse and St Patrick. Later the 'St Patrick' was dropped and the Church remained the Church of St Brisse until the new St Brycedale Free Church opened nearby in 1881, after which it became the Old Parish Kirk. In the year 2000 the two congregations combined as St Bryce Kirk.

After the Reformation the Church was abandoned as many churches were, until enough Presbyterian Ministers had been trained or retrained to lead a congregation. Early in 1800 it was

**Kirk Wynd
c1840**

**Carlyle Lodging,
Kirk Wynd**

decided that a new church should be built, however the tower, said to be of Norman origin probably dates back to the 15th Century, was retained. The old Church was described as *"the nave or body of the church is in the ancient Gothic or rather Norman style of Architecture, without buttresses, with low semicircular arches, supported by thick columns and having aisles behind them."* OSA. Adam Smith was baptised in this church on June 5 1723 and James Oswald of Dunnikier was witness. The foundation stone of the new Church was laid in 1807 by Provost John Ford who had to join the Lodge of St Brice the night before. There is a 1807 stone on the east gable of the church..

There had been a church Poor House erected in 1754 for 12 poor people which was demolished in 1806 as it was considered "too costly to maintain". It was between the main Kirk entrance and the Hendry Hall. The grassy site is fenced off and has two graves.

In the graveyard on the south wall can be seen some grave stones of the Oswald family. James Oswald (1715-69) who married Elizabeth Townsend of Warwickshire in 1746. (He is buried at Westminster Abbey) There are also several graves of people who were contemporary with Adam Smith:- Baillie Robert Philp (1751-1828); Robert Whyte (1707-96); Walter Fergus (1760-1830). The following were Provosts when Adam Smith was alive, but while buried in the Old Kirk, have no remaining headstones:- John Currie, James and Thomas Mackie, George and James Heggie, John McGill and Thomas Dougal.
**Marriage Lintel**

**220 High Street**

**Plaque**          **Adam Smith Close**

# Kirk Wynd to the High Street.

From the Old Parish Kirkyard walk down the steps, cross the road and look back at the buildings on either side of the steps.

On the left is seen the Hendry Hall built in the Scottish Baronial style and gifted to the Church by Daniel Hendry of Forth Park, manufacturer, in 1890. It shows turrets, towers, crow-step gables, date and motif. It was built on the site of the Old Trades Hall.

On the right is the old house once belonging to Matthew Anderson, maltster. It has a marriage lintel MA 1637 ML. Matthew Anderson married Margaret Law of the Merchant's House in 1637 and his coat of arms is below the initials.

Near the corner, but on Hill Street, note the plaque which states that the Burgh School was once on this site from 1725-1843. Thomas Carlyle, who taught here from 1816-18, lodged opposite (plaque on wall of Robert Nairn Licensed Restaurant). The Hill Street plaque mentions that Adam Smith and Robert Adam (1728-1795) were pupils here at about the same time. Robert Adam was born in Gladney House, which his father built for William Robertson in 1711 and in 1714 went into partnership with Robertson establishing the Linktown Brick and Tile Works. In 1716 William Adam married William Robertson's daughter Mary.

In 1795 OSA we are told that:- *"The public school is under the care of two masters, who teach in separate rooms, and without any dependence one on the other. The first master teaches Latin, French, Arithmetic, Book-Keeping and etc; the second master teaches English and Writing....... There are several private schools in the place. In all schools there are about 250 children in ordinary course of attendance."*.

# 1824 Map of Kirkcaldy little different from Smith's Day

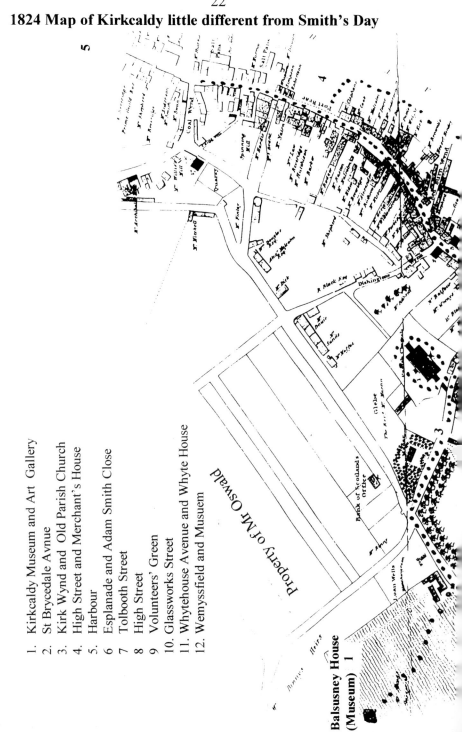

## Route of Walk

1. Kirkcaldy Museum and Art Gallery
2. St Brycedale Avnue
3. Kirk Wynd and Old Parish Church
4. High Street and Merchant's House
5. Harbour
6. Esplanade and Adam Smith Close
7. Tolbooth Street
8. High Street
9. Volunteers' Green
10. Glassworks Street
11. Whytehouse Avenue and Whyte House
12. Wemyssfield and Musuem

Balsusney House
(Museum) 1

# Plan of Adam Smith's House before reconstruction in 1834.

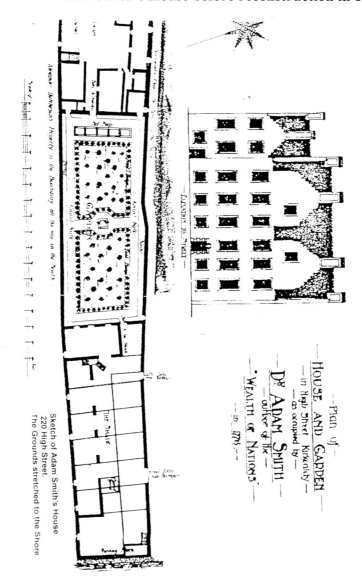

Cross over the High Street. At 220 is the site of the house that Adam Smith lived in with his mother and cousin from 1767-77. While it was rebuilt in 1834 the garden and pan-tiled, C(S) listed building at the end of the garden were there in his day as well as the nearby Adam Smith's Close that runs to the Esplanade or in those days to Sands Road. In Smith's time it was known as Halkett's Close. It is a narrow high-walled lane.

The plaque about Adam Smith at 220 High Street on the left side of the high pend built for carriages to enter, was first put up in 1919 by Kirkcaldy Naturalists and re-erected in 1953.

The long narrow gardens of the High Street properties both on the east and west side of the High Street were known as riggs. Sadly the few that remain are rarely maintained today as gardens.

**C(S) Listed building behind the Co-op Funeral Parlour.**

**Merchant's House**

**16th Century Galleon inside the house**

Adam Smith first met David Hume when he lectured in Edinburgh from 1748-51 and remained friends with him. David Hume was an avant-garde philosopher and questioned the religious dogmas of his time. He and Adam Smith corresponded frequently.

Adam Smith wrote to David Hume after his return from his Grand Tour *"My business here is study. Amusements are long solitary walks by the seaside".* Indeed Adam Smith was very much a loner. From the OSA we read that *"The sea is separated from the town by a beach of firm sand on which the inhabitants have a safe walk except at the height of the tide."*

The sea wall and Esplanade were completed in 1923 on some reclaimed land which was normally washed over only by high spring tides. As a result one can understand why high spring tides often splash over the sea wall and sometimes flood the Esplanade. The gardens of the houses on the east side of the High Street had feus that led to the High Water Mark although there was a Right of Passage along the front then known as Sands Road.

**John Paul Jones
Scots-born founder
of the American Navy
and privateer**

**Pottie's Close 1996** (Shed demolished)    **The Harbour c 1860**

# To the Harbour

Turn north along the High Street. Oswald Wynd is an old Wynd that led from the High Street to Hill Place and what is now Townsend Place. It was earlier known as Dishington Wynd, but after 1765 when James Oswald built his town house here on the High Street it was renamed Oswald's Wynd.

Turn into the blue door beside Betty Nicol's Bar (earlier known as the Victoriana) and walk into Pottie's Close. This is a very old Right of Way leading up the overgrown rigg to Hill Place near Oswald's Wynd.

In the close of 313-315, the old Pet Shop, the original bread ovens, which are listed should be visible. The property dates back to 18th Century. There was a tobacco store in an adjacent rigg.

Note the restored 16th Century Merchant's House just beyond the junction of the Esplanade and High Street. This house once belonged to the Law family and has recently been restored, having previously been known as Johnny Lena's chip shop. Later the Harbour Post Office and a Chinese Takeaway occupied the shop sites. The Merchant's House has a beautiful 17th Century plaster ceiling and a 16th Century galleon painted on an inside wall. The outside conversion was completed in 1991 but since then it has remained empty. However it is hoped that Kirkcaldy Riggs Townscape Heritage Initiative money will soon have the shops back in use with offices and flats in the rest of the building. It is anticipated that there will also be a "Kirkcaldy Room".

Further to the north is Kirkcaldy Harbour. The wet dock was built in 1843 to cope with the increase of trade and again extended in 1909. The Harbour is B listed and must remain with water. At present numerous small boats are moored in the Harbour. The non-functional dock gates remain open and so the Harbour is tidal. New flats have now been built in the Harbour area.

**Sailors' Walk c 1900**

**Bucket Patts**

*"**Effects of the Union** (1707)...this last event, whatever advantages have been ultimately derived from it to the nation at large, was long considered as an era of misfortune and distress to the trade of Scotland........duties and customs which were imposed on various articles of merchandise...contrived ... to fetter the trade of Scotland"* OSA . In fact the terms of the Union were not favourable to Scottish trade with the Continent. It was Adam Smith's father, as Controller of Customs at Kirkcaldy, who was responsible for all duties between Aberdour and Largo.

Salt production had been active in the 17th Century but dropped off due to scarcity of coal and high taxes. However around this time the industry revived. Most, if not all the salt pans on the shore were owned by Mr Oswald of Dunnikier. The bucket patts, which retained water for the salt pans when the tide went out, were retained until the building of the sea wall in 1922-23.

## Kirkcaldy Harbour

In 1760 there were only three ships at Kirkcaldy but by 1795 there were 26 square-rigged ships, 1 sloop and 2 ferry boats employing 225 men. Between 1760 and 1790, the ships between Kirkcaldy and Aberdour increased from 60 to 94.

Of Kirkcaldy the OSA states:- *"One or two of the smallest vessels are employed as coasters, and trade either to Aberdeen or London, carrying to the former, salt and coals; and to the latter the manufactures of the district; and returning from both with goods chiefly for this port and Leith......Some of the largest (ships) are then employed in the trade to the Mediterranean, the West Indies* (Slaves or convicts?) *and America.......But the greater number is employed in the trade to Holland and the Baltic. To these the only article of export is coals....chief articles imported corn, flax, flax-seed, linen yarn, wood, iron, ashes, bark, hides, tallow, cloyer-feed (clover?) apples, cheese, geniva (Holland gin) etc.."*

## High Street Bronze Table of Names

### Adam Smith wedge

"Little else is requisite to carry a state to the highest degree of opulence from the lowest barbarism, but peace, easy taxes and a tolerable administration of justice".

## Inchkeith Island

In 1778 ship-building was started, John Malcolm and the Oliphant family were among the early ship-builders in Kirkcaldy. Above Kirkcaldy Harbour rises Pathhead earlier known as Dunnikier. Here Adam Smith studied the nailers of Pathhead and used them as an example of "Manual Dexterity".

David Hume wrote to Adam Smith at this time saying *"I have a view of Kirkcaldy from my windows. I am mortally sick at Sea and regard with horror the great gulf that lies between us. There's no habitation on Inch-keith other wise I should challenge you to meet me on that spot".* He little realised that the worst part of that journey would be from Leith to Inchkeith and that from Kirkcaldy or Kinghorn, is but a short journey.

## Tolbooth Street

Turn south, walk along the Esplanade and turn up Adam Smith Close, beside the vehiclular entrance to the new Pet Shop, proceed along the High Street to Tolbooth Street.

At the top of Tolbooth Street was the Tolbooth and jail rebuilt in 1678:- *"over the Town House is the prison with separate apartments for debtors and criminals; and under it is a guard house, meal market and public weigh-house"* OSA. The Tolbooth remained here until 1826 when it moved to the High Street where it remained until 1936 when it was demolished for the new Marks and Spencer store. The Tolbooth was the centre of the town's administration and since 1953 the Town House in Wemyssfield served this purpose until 1996 when Fife Council was created and Glenrothes became the centre of Fife.

There are several attractive 18th Century houses in Tolbooth Street with dated lintels; 23-25 are B listed and dated 1785. Having been derelict they were restored in 1976 and converted to the popular Book House and Cafe. The cafe still operates as "The

**Tolbooth Street
dated lintel 1785**

**18th
Century
High
Street**

Green Parrot, Crafts and Antiques", while the Book House closed in September 2000.

**Return to the High Street**. There are two plaques on the Marks and Spencer building, one for the Tolbooth and the other the site of the Mercat Cross. There is also a paving slab on the street, indicating the site of the Cross. The Mercat Cross was regarded eventually to be deemed of "no manner of use, but a nuisance" and was taken down in 1782. It was said:-

> "Kirkcaldy pair people
> Took doon the Cross
> Tae build up a steeple"

The Mercat Cross was originally at the foot of Kirk Wynd and must have been moved at the time the Tolbooth was built in the High Street. Markets were held around the Cross and being a Royal Burgh, tradesmen from the nearby Burghs of Barony could not sell their wares here without high duties.

In 1644, even as a Royal Burgh, Kirkcaldy did not have a provost as the few councillors felt that they could cope. However the first Provost was Robert Quyt or Whyt, who became Provost in 1657. *"The government of the burgh is well vested in a Council chosen annually from three classes of inhabitants, mariners, merchants and craftsmen........the Council consists of 21 members of whom 10 must be mariners, 8 merchants and 3 craftsmen." OSA.*

Further along the High Street, at 132 is the house where Marjory Fleming, child poet, (1803-11) was born and died. While the house was built in the late 18th Century it had a new front built when it became a shop. Only by special arrangement can access be gained through the commercial car park to see the rear of the house in its original state, with its rounded storm gable facing seawards. The house is C listed.

**Pillar of Addresses**

**Old Dunnikier Church** built around 1763, enclosed by Nairn's new buildings 1901, demolished 1964.

There are three short Wynds leading off the High Street to Hill Street:- Bell Inn Wynd and Lady Inn Wynd are old wynds, while Rose Wynd is new. The entrance to the Mercat was where Adam Smith was born but the house had disappeared even before the Mercat reconstruction. Go down Charlotte Street to Volunteers' Green.

In 1644 Charles I created Kirkcaldy a Royal Burgh and at the same time gave the Common Muir or South Commonty. It was given for "the drying of linen, and taking of air in perpetuity". However successive town councils picked off and sold parts of the Green until there is now only about half an acre left in two parts. The part near the shore known as Volunteers' Green was landscaped in 1992 and the other part in Nicol Street is named Fraser's Green, after the Society's late Honorary President who did so much to save the Green from further development. The granting of Royal Burgh status absolved Kirkcaldy from paying further dues for the upkeep of Dunfermline Abbey which had been instituted in the 13th Century but the payments had lapsed since the 15th Century.

Walk back to the High Street by Glasswork Street where it is said to have been the site of Shirra Ha' built by the Rev. Shirra around 1778. Where Nicol Street joins the High Street and where the Burleigh Burn flowed from Raith lands, (now culverted) was the boundary of Linktown with Kirkcaldy.

**Walk back along the High Street, turn into Whytehouse Avenue.** This street was built for the tramcar route in 1902, turn into Park Place and walk up the Carlton entrance. Here may be seen the Whyte House built in 1790 which once had extensive grounds, but is now isolated. Cross Whytescauseway, a road since early times and continue round the back of the Town House and note the Baillies' lamps clustered together. Six burghs combined with Kirkcaldy in 1975 to form Kirkcaldy District. There should be seven lamps:- Kirkcaldy, Kinghorn, Burntisland, Methil and

Buckhaven, Leven, Leslie and Markinch, but the one from Leslie is missing.

**Return to Kirkcaldy Museum and Art Gallery**, if open look at the small collection of Adam Smith artefacts including both the first and fourth edition of the "Wealth of Nations" published in Adam Smith's lifetime. There are also copies in Korean and German. **Rear of the house where Marjory Fleming lived and died.**

Reverse / Kirkcaldy penny of Scotland 1797

## Adam Smith Stamp 1973

**Medallion 1787** by Tassie said by Dugald Stewart to be a 'good likeness'.There was also an Adam Smith penny minted for private collectors only. This had the Tassie head on one side and symbols of industry, done by Jacques Turgot 1876 (France), on the other.

## CanongateChurch
Edinburgh

**"Welcome to Kirkcaldy"**
before 1998 and after.
**Also Historic Board**

**Baillies'
Lamps**

# Important Dates of Adam Smith's Life

| | |
|---|---|
| 1723 | Baptised in Kirkcaldy Church |
| 1737-40 | University Student Glasgow |
| 1740-46 | Student at Oxford |
| 1748-51 | Lectured in Edinburgh |
| 1752-63 | Chair of Logic and Moral Philosophy, Glasgow |
| 1764-67 | Continental Grand Tour as Tutor |
| 1767-73 | In Kirkcaldy |
| 1773-1777 | Mainly London |
| 1776 | First Edition of Wealth of Nations, published. |
| 1777-90 | Commissioner of Customs, Scotland, Edinburgh |
| 1790 | Died, buried Canongate Kirkyard. |

# National Events during Adam Smith's Life

| | |
|---|---|
| 1714-1727 | George I |
| 1727-1760 | George II |
| 1760-1820 | George III |

| | |
|---|---|
| 1733 | Secession of the Church against Patronage. |
| 1745-46 | Highland Jacobite Uprising defeated. |
| 1752 | Britain adopts Gregorian Calendar, loses 11 days. |
| 1756-63 | Seven Years War. Germany and Britain against France and Austria. |
| 1762 | Catherine (II) the Great, became ruler of Russia. |
| 1773 | Boston Tea Party. |
| 1775-76 | American War of Independence. |
| 1785 | Italian Balloonist, Lunardi, lands in Fife (Ceres). |
| 1789-92 | French Revolution. |

| | |
|---|---|
| 1759-96 | Robert Burns |

12 Scots pounds = one English pound

# Significant Records, mostly from Kirkcaldy Burgh Minutes by Lachlan Macbean

| | |
|---|---|
| 1734 | Proposed to pull down the Mercat Cross and dig a public well here instead. John Brymer to enquire cost of lead pipe from School Well and Manse Well to the Cross. |
| 1736 | Andrew Wilson hanged in Edinburgh for murder of Customs Officer in Pittenweem. His partner in crime Andrew Robertson escaped. |
| 1740 | 11 children killed when the Pathhead Cave collapsed on Handsel Monday. |
| 1741 | Mr James Oswald becomes Kirkcaldy's MP. |
| 1742 | Council levies 2 Scots pence per pint ale/beer for 25 years!! |
| 1744 | Council acts to stop smuggling from the Continent especially of brandy. |
| 1745 | Had to pay Jacobites for repairs to Holyrood and billeting of troops in town. |
| 1748 | No yarn to be sold at markets before 8 in the morning. |
| 1749 | John Wilson, brewer appointed to clean streets of middings twice a week. He kept the dung. |
| 1750 | Roup of South Commonty. |
| 1752 | Harbour damaged by storm. Pier to be built on west side to keep saltpans free of sand and "danders".(cinders) |
| 1753 | Two Forth ferry boats; first in to get first berth. |
| 1753 | Owing to danger to children, riding in carts through the town is not to be permitted, horses must be led. |
| 1770 | Storm damage to harbour. |
| 1774 | First water supply from "Latch" to street well. |
| 1778 | Harbour wrecked. again. |
| 1782 | Coastal towns prepare for defence. Cross removed. |
| 1785 | Lamps purchased for streets from sale of dung. |

# Death of Andrew Wilson and the Porteous Riots 1736

Andrew Wilson was a baker from Kirkcaldy who with his friend Andrew Robertson had intended to steal money from the hated Customs Officer at Pittenweem, but they accidentally killed him. They were caught, arrested, tried in Edinburgh and sentenced to death. On their last Sunday they were taken to church, Robertson managed to escape while Andrew Wilson caused a diversion. Robertson was never caught but Wilson was hanged in the Grassmarket in Edinburgh in 1736. The crowd rioted and Captain Porteous illegally ordered the soldiers to fire on the crowd. He was detained but later the crowd broke in, took him and hanged him from a dye-staff in the Grassmarket. Andrew Wilson's grave is in Kirkcaldy Pathhead Feuars' graveyard, erected by Public Subscription. On the stone it says that "his name was associated with the genius of Sir W. Scott and the Porteous mob".

Adam Smith would have been 13 at this time.

**Grave of Andrew Wilson**

**Clydesdale Bank of Scotland £50**